Education:
Roast & Toast

Education: Roast & Toast

Anecdotes of 60+ Years of Teaching

Diane T. Martin, MEd,
and
Linda V. Thomas, BA

Edited by Ellen M. Martin

iUniverse, Inc.
Bloomington

Education: Roast & Toast
Anecdotes of 60+ Years of Teaching

iUniverse books may be ordered through booksellers or by contacting:

iUniverse
1663 Liberty Drive
Bloomington, IN 47403
www.iuniverse.com
1-800-Authors (1-800-288-4677)

ISBN: 978-1-4620-2833-7 (sc)
ISBN: 978-1-4620-2835-1 (hc)
ISBN: 978-1-4620-2834-4 (ebk)

Printed in the United States of America

iUniverse rev. date: 10/31/2011

Contents

To our favorite colleagues

(and you know who you are, don't you?)

DOCENTS' LIMERICK

There once were two spirited teachers,
Who reminisced and talked like preachers.
They gave up the small chatter
And wrote something of matter,
So, let's take a look at the keepers.

PREFACE

Education: Roast & Toast offers a unique behind-the-scenes glimpse of gaffes and goofs by those involved in public school education. It is surprising, laughable, and, of course, *learningful.*

Since snickers and giggles infused our teaching days, we talked about what prompted this humor and joked about writing a book of anecdotes after we retired.

It wasn't long before the joking became serious conversation. We discussed the *faux pas* we had gathered, knowing that our colleagues would appreciate these gaffes, too.

From the beginning of *Education: Roast & Toast,* we wrote tongue-in-cheek, allowing educators to be seen as we are—eccentric, imperfect, and vulnerable, in spite of degrees, knowledge, and experience.

For years we were neighbors, teaching across the hall from each other—Martin, English; Thomas, French. Between classes, we converged for mini-faculty meetings with other teachers in the hallway. At lunch and after school, we "cussed" and discussed the *backward evolution* of education. Saving entertaining and funny e-mails and notes; clipping ridiculous newspaper and magazine articles; and recalling random conversations gave birth to ideas for *Education: Roast & Toast*. We laughed *at* ourselves and *with* our colleagues without losing sight of the seriousness of teaching.

Inspired by the humor of sixty-plus years of education experience, we began diligently and purposefully reviewing everything we had accumulated. That took us to the realization that administrators, students, and parents would also enjoy these collective foibles since these individuals were equally responsible. The time had come to compile the mish-mash into manageable segments.

We threw out more than we kept. We forgot more than we included. We emphasized student slip-ups to reveal the often-humorous interaction between student and teacher. We embellished teacher, administrator, and parent goofs to set the tone for what is included in our writing.

Crossing from our writing comfort zones into unfamiliar territory was a strenuous challenge. This demanding task was softened, however, by our laughter while working with humorous anecdotes: a *learningful* week, *backward evolution,* and *horse choking,* readily come to mind.

Education: Roast & Toast begins with "All in a Day's Work," allowing the reader to eavesdrop on a teacher's world. Another segment, "Uhh … Huh?" gives pause to wonder where the intelligentsia are. A few scenarios highlight "Signs of the Times," leading us into "Great Expectations," which spans over one hundred years. *Education: Roast & Toast* even lets you determine whether "[y]ou Might Be a Schoolteacher …" or not. Finally, a section of oxymoronic anecdotes reflects a "Backward Evolution" in education.

Laughter is said to be good for the soul; therefore, our souls are in great shape. We hope this is a workout for yours as well.

Diane T. Martin, MEd, and
Linda V. Thomas, BA
April 11, 2011

ACKNOWLEDGMENTS

Thank you, educators and former students who gave us the impetus to attempt this project.

We are especially appreciative of these talented individuals whose aphorisms contribute to our spirited tales of a "learningful" profession: Stanley Crochet, a local city policeman; Raynesha Dewey, a day-care worker; David Hymel, a PhD candidate in medicinal chemistry; and Tuong Pham, a future pharmacist.

We are grateful to Judy Broussard, an avid reader of varied genres, and Ginger Gaubert, a former high school English teacher, for reading and critiquing our book in its infancy.

Without the editorial direction of our publisher, iUniverse, our book would not be what we had envisioned.

Finally, we are most indebted to our friend Ellen M. Martin who untiringly mentored us in the appropriate rhetoric by constantly urging and challenging us to improve *Education: Roast & Toast.* Writing this book would have been more difficult without Ellen's professional knowledge, expertise, and, most of all, spontaneous humor that kept us focused. Because of her "cracking the whip" and motivating us to dig deeper, we achieved a level of humor we never knew we had. Her persistence forced us to look at our writing through a different perspective and made us realize she was more often right than not. Ellen, we can never thank you enough.

Merci beaucoup!

ALL IN A DAY'S WORK

"A story is not a story without
someone telling it."

—Raynesha Dewey (2000)

Duty Calls:

The twenty-first century has taught teachers a new meaning for the anti-drug slogan "Say no to crack"—as a dress code reminder.

TEACHER: Are those *slippers*, Miss Jones?

Pink shirt, Sir?

Are you pregnant, Young Man? *Untucked shirts* are only allowed for pregnant students.

Now come **the look** and **the question**: "Ya talkin' ta me?"

Humor is a panacea for morning duty!

Rringgg! Time for class.
Ils sont partis!

"The Sky Is Falling! The Sky Is Falling!"

ASSISTANT PRINCIPAL:

Fights took place today.

IDs were not visible.

Duty teachers were everywhere but unaware.

Walk! Look! Listen! ID all students.

Culprits are still at large!

Copy that, Chicken Little!

"Non-Answering"—
Principal Style:

TEACHER: Why don't classrooms get cold air from the A/C?

PRINCIPAL: When we kids wasted food, my grandma used to say, "Think of all those starving children in China." Well, think of all the people who don't have air conditioning.

TEACHER: If you ate all your food, did the children in China feel full? And if I think of people who have no A/C, will I be cool?

More hot air!

All in a Day's Work:

TEACHER: Mrs. Mó Néy, Ja' Maka can't read and can't write. It seems she has been placed in the wrong grade.

MRS. MÓ NÉY: I think I need to take her back to that doctor. It's gotta be her medicine.

Medical miracle!

~

Our Little Secret:

FROM: Mrs. John Brown

TO: Ms. Martin

We're going to the beach this weekend, so Bobby won't be at school Monday.

Please don't teach anything new because he already studied for his test on Tuesday.

P.S. Don't tell him about this e-mail. He'd be embarrassed.

Freudian Slip of the Finger?

PRINCIPAL'S MEMO: There will be a faculty meeting during conference block tomorrow.

After reading this, the teacher thought she would forward a gripe about the memo to a colleague:

TEACHER: I can't believe the principal's still doing this! Why doesn't he give us advanced notice about these @#!! meetings?

The next morning the teacher was horrified when she opened her e-mail to see this return message:

PRINCIPAL: Shhh … He might hear you.

P.A.'s in the A.M.:

PRINCIPAL: FYI, CST has changed to CDT. Seniors, take SSNs and IDs to ACT and SAT practice at LSU.

That's a 10-4.

Interruptions Are Taxing:

RECEPTIONIST OVER P.A.:

Excuse me, your *e-ternal* revenue

man's here again.

**"… [Y]esterday, and today,
and forever."**

—Hebrews 13:8

Teachers' Daily Duty:

ASSISTANT PRINCIPAL:

Send your *absentees* to the office.

Sheer genius!

UHH ... HUH?

"Don't flirt with Death because he just might kiss you."

—Stanley Crochet (1998)

Profound Proclamation from Principal:

When you know in advance you will be out sick on a given day, call the assistant principal ASAP so she can locate a substitute.

If we knew *this*, we could hang our shingle: "Sister Diane & Sister Linda, clairvoyants for hire."

A Student Speculated on a "Ponderful" Idea:

STUDENT: Oh, wow! It'd be awesome if the Ides of March fell on Friday the thirteenth.

TEACHER: And if the Fourth of July fell on Cinco de Mayo, we'd have another school holiday!

OMG!

Knock, Knock.
Who's There?

PRINCIPAL: Please knock my door in the hallway.

Huh?

Alert During
Fire Prevention Week:

PRINCIPAL: When there's a fire, students and faculty should remain in class with doors closed.

What'd he say?

~

Wheel of Fortune
Candidate?

STUDENT: Madame Thomas, would ya take off for misspelled words on vocabulary quizzes?

MADAME THOMAS: Of course! If you misspell the word in French or English, it's incorrect!

STUDENT: For just *one letter?*

Reflex Humor:

ATHLETE: Coach, what's wrong with your shoulder? Is that jerking involuntary?

COACH: Nah, it jus' does it by itself.

Some things just shouldn't be repeated.

College English Professors Should Practice What They Profess: Proofread! Proofread! Proofread!

DEPARTMENT CHAIR: It makes no sense whatsoever that a student should return to class by a teacher who has completed the course.

So, this is higher ed.?

After a Week Studying *Macbeth,* a Student Was Overheard Saying to Her Teacher ...

That was *hard*! But, it was a *learningful* week.

"Double, double, toil and trouble …"

Circumvention of Circumstances Leads to a Circle:

When asked about a transfer student's present grades not reflecting those from his previous school, the guidance counselor replied, "I understand there were *insinuating* circumstances."

Oops!

Vocabulary Grand Slam:

Jane to Mary: Did you see that home run Dozar hit yesterday? It was *superfluous*!

And it was *good*, too!

GREAT EXPECTATIONS

"The best laid schemes o' mice an' men/Gang aft agley."

—Robert Burns (1785)

School Board Expectations—
1872 and 2010:

1872: Every teacher should lay aside from each pay a goodly sum of his earnings for his benefit during his declining years so that he will not become a burden on society.

2010: Teachers will have a goodly sum removed from their earnings to support future *non-tenured* teachers who would become burdens on society.

1872: Teachers each day will fill lamps, clean slates, bring a bucket of water, and a scuttle of coal for the day's session.

2010: Teachers who clean their classrooms daily will be reported to the principal for infringement of custodial duties.

More Expectations:

1872: After ten hours in school, the teachers may spend the remaining time reading the Bible or other good books.

2010: After seven hours of teaching, teachers may then go to the restroom.

1872: Teachers who perform their labor faithfully and without fault for five years will be given an increase of twenty-five cents per week in their pay, providing the Board of Education approves.

2010: Teachers who perform their labor faithfully and without fault for five years will receive free and unlimited lifetime psychiatric care.

49

And Even More:

1872: Male teachers may take one evening each week for courting purposes, or two evenings a week if they go to church regularly.

2010: Male teachers may party on the weekend if they sponsor the school's **GPA.***

1872: Male teachers who smoke, use liquor in any form, frequent pool or public halls, or get shaved in a barber shop will give good reason to suspect their worth, intention, and integrity.

2010: Male teachers who have no extracurricular fun will become suspect.

***GPA: Governor's Program on Abstinence**

51

Some More:

1872: Female teachers may not dye their hair.

2010: Female teachers who dye their hair must tell the truth about their ages.

1872: Female teachers who marry or engage in unseemly conduct will be dismissed.

2010: Female teachers should earnestly search for a mate with whom to combine salaries to make ends meet. (Pun intended.)

And One More:

1872: Teachers may not travel beyond the city limits, unless previous permission has been granted by the chairman of the Board of Education.

2010: Some educational rules never change, just the reasons—same rule!

Assistant Principal
Investigates Horseplay:

Vasel' Ine Hines's mother came to school this morning concerning the incident that took place on Friday. She was upset with you for allegedly *horse choking* her son because he didn't say, "Good morning."

I assured her your intentions were good and that you don't *horse choke* your students. She wanted to see the incident on camera, but I didn't allow it.

I checked the tape after she left, but the area where it happened is a blind spot for the camera.

By the way, what the hell is "horse choking"?

Administrator's
Faux Pas:

"Earlier today I inadvertently sent out a **confidential document** along with the secretarial advertisement.

"Please destroy any confidential information you received and **do not** divulge or discuss its contents."

Too late! It's viral.

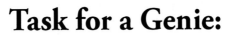

Task for a Genie:

ASSISTANT PRINCIPAL:

Some of you expressed interest in having a color-coded Crisis Response sheet. *If you don't have one and would like one laminated, please print it out and send it to me.*

Abra-ca-dabra …

"Customized" or Not?

Teachers asked if a $250,000 "customized" electronic grade book could drop the confusing "Saturday column" which wasn't being used.

The Central Office response was, "Do you think it was customized just for *us*?"

Well, yeahh!

Teacher's Note to Principal:

"If perchance after school, a janitor is strolling the halls, checking for unlocked doors, he could accidentally (or not) lock the restroom door with a teacher inside!

"We had always taken for granted that the restroom keys would work, not only to lock the door from the outside but also to unlock the door from the inside, in case someone were accidentally (or not) locked in."

However, an experiment one afternoon proved otherwise.

Shortly thereafter, the principal was locked accidentally (or not) in the men's restroom upstairs. Locks were changed!

. . . end of story.

SIGNS OF THE TIMES

"Life lets you walk the road;

education gives you a car."

—David Hymel (2003)

Scenario 1: Hunting

Jack goes rabbit hunting before school and then pulls into the school parking lot with his shotgun in his truck's gun rack.

1960: Assistant principal walks over, looks at Jack's shotgun, goes to his own truck, and gets *his* shotgun to show Jack.

2010: School goes into lockdown, FBI called, Jack hauled off to jail and never sees his truck or gun again. Counselors called in for traumatized students and teachers.

from Friend to Foe ...

Scenario 2: Fighting

Frankie and Johnny get into a fist fight after school.

1960: Crowd gathers. Frankie wins. Frankie and Johnny shake hands and end up buddies.

2010: Police called. SWAT team arrives. Frankie and Johnny are arrested and charged with assault. Both are expelled, even though Johnny started it.

from Drama to Trauma …

~

Scenario 3: Running

Charlie falls while running during recess and scrapes her knee. Mr. Smith, her teacher, comforts her with a hug when he finds her crying.

1960: In a short time, Charlie feels better and goes on playing.

2010: Mr. Smith is accused of being a sexual predator and loses his job. He faces three years in state prison. Charlie undergoes five years of therapy and wins a substantial settlement from the school board.

from Hugs to Shrugs ...

Scenario 4: Sharing

Fred takes his favorite camp tool to class.

1960: Fred demonstrates his Swiss Army knife for Show-'n-Tell and uses it to eat his lunch.

2010: The folding knife is banned as a dangerous instrument under the school district's zero tolerance policy. Six-year-old Fred faces forty-five days' expulsion for "camp tool violation," and the story becomes a national media sensation. NBC's *Today* and CBS's *The Early Show* interview the first grader and his mother.

from Demonstration to Violation ...

Effective Study Habits?

Squirming in his desk and shielding his eyes with his hand throughout a test, the student was questioned by the teacher about this suspect behavior.

STUDENT: I don't cheat! I don't lie! I'm a Christian!

When he slapped his paper, emphasizing his innocence, his sweaty palm left an imprint of the answers as obvious evidence of his guilt.

Amen!

~

Re-Search 'n Rescue:

TEACHER: What did you think of the literary analysis?

STUDENT: What's that?

TEACHER: Your *research paper*—a literary analysis.

STUDENT: *Our* research paper?

His Story:

TEACHER: How's your summer vacation going?

STUDENT: Ah—not so good. I gotta go to summer school 'cause my teacher didn't like me.

TEACHER: As if ...

STUDENT: She said I was the class clown!

TEACHER: And?

STUDENT: History just ain't that funny.

TEACHER: But it does have a way of repeating itself, doesn't it?

NCLB* Law …
Dumbing It Down:

---

*NCLB: No Child Left Behind

Conversation between two eighth graders:

STUDENT A: Did you study for that big, long test?

STUDENT B: Nuh-uh. Why?

STUDENT A: Don' cha wanna do good?

STUDENT B: It don' matta. I'll pass anyways.

STUDENT A: Nuh-uh, not if ya don' make the right grade; they'll fail ya.

STUDENT B: So? I'll jus' go ta summer school. It'll be easier.

STUDENT A: How do ya know that?

STUDENT B: All o' my brothers went.

Misleading Headlines:

"Student Arrested for Taking Ax to School"

a. "Student" is five years old.

b. "Ax" is plastic and five inches long.

c. "School" is a kindergarten class.

~

Misleading-*er*:

"Student Arrested for Sexual Harassment and Pagan Ritual"

a. "Student" is a third grader.

b. "Harassment" is a kiss given to another third grader.

c. "Pagan ritual" is Valentine's Day.

~

Misleading-*est*:

"US Students on Top"

a. "US Students" is United States high school teenagers.

b. "on Top" as in human reproduction. (Pun intended!)

YOU MIGHT BE A
SCHOOLTEACHER ...

"A student is not a student without

the help of a teacher."

—Raynesha Dewey (2000)

You Might Be a Schoolteacher
If ...

~

… you tend to *question the DNA* between parent and child.

… you are compelled to *decorate a family bulletin board* for the change of seasons.

… you hang around the public library and *ask for free bookmarks.*

You Might Be a Schoolteacher When ...

… you hoard pencils *with or without erasers.*

… you receive *more gifts in a single school year* than most children get throughout adolescence.

… you laugh uncontrollably at someone referring to the Teachers' Lounge as a "*workroom.*"

You Might Be a Schoolteacher
As Long As …

… you can *distinguish* among Code Red, Code Blue, Code Green, Code Fushia, Code Tangerine, Code Yellow, and Code Magenta, and can *remember* the password for each.

… you can *decipher* all handwriting.

… you tell anyone who slouches, "Sit up straight."

You Might Be a Schoolteacher

Because …

… your family gatherings are conducted like *committee meetings* and summer vacations are organized like *field trips.*

… you wonder, *"Where do all these gifted children come from?"* and *"Where do they go after gifted class?"*

… your dream is to invent a *button-activated odor eliminator* in the classroom ceiling.

You Might Be a Schoolteacher
Since ...

... you guard your *secret code* to operate the copy machine as though it were a PIN for an ATM.

... you become nauseated when you hear the phrase *cafeteria duty.*

... you can retire by fencing your *stockpile of school supplies* on the black market.

Gal Pal Exchange:

RETIRED TEACHER: Would October 19th or 26th be better to meet you after school?

ACTIVE TEACHER: Sure. Do you want to come after school?

Whew! Retired—just in time!

Reading Between the Lines (As Usual):

PRINCIPAL: I'm sure you know how I feel about e-mails in this tone.

Your tone or my tone?

ADD* at Its Best:

*A.D.D.: Attention Deficit Disorder

~

Sally sat, clicking nails on desk, propping chin on hand, staring at the door in anticipation of dismissal. Others whispered while some rolled their eyes and passed notes. Even though this is commonplace in school, today it was mind boggling!

These were teachers at a faculty meeting!

Educators Heart Acronyms:

PRINCIPAL: Please fill out this EOY survey. The COC expects it by EOM.

TEACHER: EOY … EOM … This is February. It's not the end of the year.

PRINCIPAL: FYI, you can C&P from last year's survey, ASAP.

Red-Inked
Typos and Slip-Ups:

"Books help students build much better *potfolios*."

Chaucer's "An Old Wives' *Tail*" encourages students to read.

"School Board *erection* finally over."

BACKWARD EVOLUTION

"Failures r the 1 way 2 teach the
importance of successes."

—Tuong Pham (2005)

Six of One, Half a Dozen of the Other:

CUSTOMER: I'd like half a dozen chicken nuggets.

TEENAGE FAST-FOOD

EMPLOYEE: You can't order half a dozen. It's six, nine, or twelve."

CUSTOMER: So, I can order *six,* but not half a dozen?

EMPLOYEE: Yeah!

This **must be the** *new math!*

Forbidden "Fruit":

TEACHER: Joan, did you lose your strawberry?

JOAN: My *what?*

TEACHER: You know, your *strawberry,* your *strawberry!*

JOAN: What are you *talking* about?

TEACHER: That thing you talk on ... your cell phone.

JOAN: Ahh ... You mean my *Blackberry!*

~

Mumbo Jumbo:

PRINCIPAL: Too many teachers are sitting at their computers during instructional time. This should stop immediately!

However, if you receive e-mail from the *office*, be sure to handle *that* right away.

There's one for the spam folder!

Progressive Regression:

In a letter to parents/guardians: Our records indicate that your child is *in danger of FAIL-URE because of ATTENDANCE.*

Students will definitely take this message home!

Electronic Intervention:

Help! The computer doesn't recognize acronyms!

It has rejected the BRA from the name of our teachers' organization (BRA+PEL*).

Don't you think tossing the BRA is needless?

We must keep the BRA for support!

---

*BRA+PEL: **Baton Rouge Association for Professional Educators of Louisiana**

Banter Referring to a Previous Awards Ceremony Was Computer-Censored Due to Sexual Content:

ASSISTANT PRINCIPAL: Hey, just wanted to congratulate all you teachers on a job well done last night, and thanks for helping make the ceremony a success.

TEACHER A: I heard we were all nominated for an Oscar.

TEACHER B: Is that an Oscar Mayer?

TEACHER C: I heard it was an Oscar de la Renta!

TEACHER B: I'd rather the *wiener*.

TEACHER A : You're already a *hot dog*.

"Gen X"

Lesson plans for *Julius Caesar* have changed to accommodate differentiated learning styles through the years:

1960: Class, you must memorize and recite Marc Antony's *entire oration* after the death of Julius Caesar, *thirty-five lines.* The recitation, from the podium, will be delivered at the end of the week, on Friday. **(35 points; a separate grade from the Unit Test; on the UT you will *write a short essay* explaining irony and how it is shown in this speech)**

~

"Gen X" cont'd

1970: You must memorize and recite *part of Marc Antony's oration* after the death of Julius Caesar, the first *twenty-five lines.* Begin at "Friends, ..." and end at "Was this ambition?" This is due one week from today. You may stand by your desk to recite. **(12.5 points for the memory work and 12.5 points for explaining the irony used in the speech, *written in a paragraph* on the Unit Test)**

"Me" Generation

1980: You must learn and recite the first *fifteen lines* of Marc Antony's oration after the death of Julius Caesar. Begin at "Friends, …" and end at "And Brutus is an honorable man." This memory work will be due at the end of our reading the play, *a week and a half.* You may sit at your desk to recite the lines. Some of you have inquired about *reciting in rap style*; you may do this, but you will have to recite at the front of the classroom. There is no extra credit for rap. **(30 points—2 points per line)**

1990: You will be responsible for learning the *first two lines* of Marc Antony's speech after the death of Julius Caesar. Begin at "Friends, …" and end at "… praise him." This will appear on the Unit Test, and you will have to *fill in the blanks, using a word bank.* **(14 points—2 points per answer; 2 points for getting answers in correct order)**

"Net Gen"

2000: You will be *responsible for identifying the first line* of Marc Antony's speech after the death of Julius Caesar. The line begins "Friends, …" and ends "ears[.]" **(Because I changed the punctuation, I had to put my change into brackets; you will find a semicolon here in the speech. Don't use this as an excuse that you couldn't find the right line.)** This will be a *matching item.* **(2 points for the correct match)**

2010: (1) After *watching a video* of **Julius Caesar** and *partially reading* this play, you will need to know the playwright **(the person who wrote the play)** and

(2) the *name of the character* who said, "Friends, Romans, countrymen, …"

(3) The Unit Test will be *four weeks* from today.

(4) You will be given an *act-by-act study guide* to help you learn about the characters and the action of this drama **(play)**.

(5) Each part of the answer will be 2 points; however, if both are right, your paper will receive 5 *extra points*.

(6) Begin studying **now**.

AUTHORS' THOUGHTS

We're done! We heart you all.

—Diane and Linda (2011)

Authors' Thoughts

Reflecting on **Education: Roast & Toast** gives us new insight into how crucial laughter is to living, learning, and surviving. A hundred years ago, laughter in the classroom was a rarity, usually at the expense of someone else. Today, teacher and student laugh together at yesterday's strict and forbidding pedagogy and discuss the difficulties one had to overcome in order to learn.

Yesterday's classroom concentrated on the framing of America. Modern curricula are significantly enhanced by technologies encompassing students' lifestyles, including the media, Internet, video games, mass communication, and the Information Age. Workforce situations are simulated through cooperative learning in classrooms. These learning situations are necessary for the choices of and opportunities for the myriad career fields educators envision.

Today's educators are able to anticipate the distant future. Many are better prepared due to receiving master's degrees before leaving university. Educators continue professional development through workshops, computer conferencing, and interdisciplinary training. They enlighten students for future challenges.

Through sixty-plus years, certainly there were times when we were disheartened because our students were frustrated or disinterested. But the number of teaching years proves we never lost enthusiasm for our goal to educate.

Change is usually frightening and uncomfortable, and *so much* in education has changed … *but* for the better.

dtm & lvt
April 11, 2011

~

"Man is the only creature endowed
with the power of laughter; …
[except for the hyena]."

—Lord Greville, English poet

CPSIA information can be obtained at www.ICGtesting.com
Printed in the USA
BVOW031527171111

276231BV00005B/122/P